New Testament Textual Criticism

A Concise Guide

David Alan Black

D0144821

Baker Books

A Division of Baker Book House Co
Grand Rapids, Michigan 49516

© 1994 by David Alan Black

Published by Baker Books
a division of Baker Book House Company
P.O. Box 6287, Grand Rapids, MI 49516-6287

Third printing, October 1999

Printed in the United States of America

ISBN:0-8010-1074-8

Cataloging-in-Publication Data on file
at the Library of Congress, Washington, D.C.

To
Dr. Bernhard Wyss
Professor Emeritus of Greek Philology
at the University of Basel,
who, in the tradition of Erasmus,
taught me the joy of
New Testament textual criticism

Contents

Preface and Acknowledgments

A. T. Robertson, the famous Greek scholar, once called the Greek New Testament "the Torchbearer of Light and Progress for the world" (*The Minister and His Greek New Testament*, p. 116). If this is true (and it is), then any light we can shed *on* the text of the New Testament ought to help us gain light *from* it.

Unfortunately, many Christians have never had the opportunity to learn even the basics about New Testament textual criticism—the study of the original wording of the New Testament. Recently, in a church in Hawaii, a bright young pastor came up to me and said, "I have some people who are quite fanatical about the King James Version. They say it is based on the 'best' Greek texts. I know that others in my congregation disagree. Can you help me?" This pastor wasn't alone in his dilemma. I have met many others like him in churches large and small. They wonder, for example, why the King James Version includes the confession of the Ethiopian eunuch (Acts 8:37) and the doxology of the Lord's Prayer (Matt. 6:13), while the New International Version does not.

I wrote this book for people like that young pastor and his congregation in Hawaii. It represents material I have presented to literally hundreds of pastors and lay persons in Bible-teaching workshops. In a sense, this book packages up those workshops and delivers them in a readily accessible form. You might call it a "teach yourself" clinic. And you can either work through it on your own or use it to guide a group study.

Like its predecessors *Linguistics for Students of New Testament Greek* (Grand Rapids: Baker, 1988), *Using New Testament Greek in Ministry* (Grand Rapids: Baker, 1993), and *Learn to Read New Testament Greek* (Nashville: Broadman, 1993), this volume attempts to make the findings of scholarship accessible to a wide readership. Nothing in this book has been taken for granted. Every term, every problem, is explained clearly, concisely, and "from scratch." If you want to use a more detailed introduction to textual criticism alongside the present book, I recommend Bruce M. Metzger's *The Text of the New Testament* (3d rev. ed.; Oxford: University Press, 1992), the standard in this field. However, lest I convey the impression that the present volume was written only for persons who are new to the task of Bible study, let me say that it will also serve as a good refresher course for those who have been in the business for a while. When I played college basketball (two decades and several pounds ago), our coach insisted that we constantly practice the fundamentals—dribbling, passing, shooting, running. Likewise, I've discovered the value of reviewing the basics of good Bible study. And, while the fundamentals are covered in this book, I am confident you will also pick up some new ideas along the way.

As you read the following chapters, you will notice that they build upon each other. Chapter 1 contains an overview of the "raw materials" needed to do New Testament textual criticism. Chapter 2 describes the history of textual criticism and continues with a consideration of the criteria scholars use to evaluate variant readings. Chapter 3 offers a few brief hints on how to work through a textual problem on your own and provides several examples of that process. As you master these chapters, take any opportunity you can to teach them to someone else. This will increase your own understanding and that of your congregation or Bible study group.

It now remains to express a word of deep appreciation to the many persons who in one way or another have given me kind encouragement and have made suggestions for the improvement of this book. In the first place, I wish to acknowledge the patience of my students at Talbot School of Theology, Simon Greenleaf University, Grace Bible Institute, and various other locations, who worked with the material in syllabus form and gave me their honest reactions to the text. I am particularly indebted to two outstanding Talbot students, Mrs. Terri Butts and Mr. Chiao Ek Ho, for scrutinizing the manuscript in detail. In addition, it has been a pleasure to have once again the fine services of Allan Fisher, Jim Weaver, and Maria denBoer as my editors at Baker Book House. Their friendly, efficient, and often crucial help has made the writing of this book a joy. My final thanks go to my former teachers in New

Testament textual criticism: the late Dr. Harry Sturz of Biola University, and Dr. Berhard Wyss of the University of Basel. To the latter, who patiently taught me to read Greek minuscule handwriting and kindly gave me access to the Greek manuscripts in the University Library, this book is dedicated with affectionate and abiding gratitude.

1

Scribes, Scrolls, and Scripture

The Purpose and Materials of New Testament Textual Criticism

Introduction

This book is a simple and direct introduction to New Testament textual criticism—the study of the original text of the New Testament. It is dedicated to the principle that an understanding of this subject is possible for all students of the Bible. Its aim is to take inquirers behind the dust of scholarship to the living faith that pulsates in the New Testament documents.

My purpose in this chapter is modest. I will discuss the kinds of writing materials that were available in the ancient world and provide some information about the kinds of evidence we use to recover the original text. However, it seems best at the outset to say something about the importance and scope of the text-critical task.

The Importance and Scope of New Testament Textual Criticism

The importance of New Testament textual criticism is best seen in its purpose: to recover the original text of the New Testament from the available evidence. Two factors make New Testament textual criticism a necessary field of study. The first is that none of the original manuscripts (often called the "autographs") of the New Testament has survived. No one can say why this is so—except that a sovereign God designed it that way. Perhaps if an autograph had survived, it would have been worshiped or even exploited as a relic. More probably the originals were worn out after repeated reading, both private and public.

The second reason why textual criticism is necessary is because there are numerous mistakes in the extant copies of the New Testament. These mistakes must be identified, and the correct reading deduced, before exegesis can take place. New Testament textual criticism is, therefore, basic to all other biblical and theological study. Interpretation, teaching, and preaching cannot be done until textual criticism has done its work.

Before discussing the materials available to the New Testament textual critic, I must say something about the scope of the text-critical task. In the first place, it is essential to keep in mind that the great majority of variants (instances of different wording) between manuscripts are of relatively minor importance. These generally involve such matters as spelling or word order, which minimally affect translation or the sense of the text. Analogous instances of variation in English would include the spelling of "center/centre" and "labor/labour."

Second, however, it must be admitted that the New Testament manuscripts do contain numerous significant variants. These variants number around two thousand, the majority of which are carefully discussed in Bruce M. Metzger's *A Textual Commentary on the Greek New Testament*—an indispensable resource for New Testament students. Some of these variants are more important than others, but most of them affect translation and interpretation in some way. For example, in John 3:13 some manuscripts read "the Son of Man who is in heaven," implying that Jesus was in heaven while speaking to Nicodemus, while other manuscripts omit the clause "who is in heaven." This is considered a "significant" variant because it has an important bearing on Christology (see the discussion of this variant in Chapter 3). Of course, such variants should not overshadow the overwhelming degree of agreement that exists among the ancient manuscripts. In fact, the most important differences in today's English New Testament are due, not to textual variation, but to the way translators view their task (i.e., paraphrase versus literal translation).

Finally, it is a lamentable fact that New Testament textual critics remain seriously divided over the criteria to be used in the selection of the most likely original reading. These criteria fall broadly into two classes: one class emphasizes "external evidence"—the age, grouping, and distribution of the manuscripts; the other, "internal evidence"—the habits of scribes (copyists) and the peculiarities (both stylistic and doctrinal) of the author. The ambiguity of these criteria makes New Testament textual criticism an art as much as a science, and conclusions regarding any particular variant reading are often the result of a tenuous balance of criteria for or against it.

Writing Materials in the Ancient World

Before studying specific kinds of textual variants, it will be helpful to become acquainted with some details of paleography, the study of ancient writing. In antiquity a great variety of materials were used to receive writing. Waxed tablets, comprised of a piece of wood coated with wax, were used in Greece and Rome from earliest times. Such a tablet was probably used by Zechariah, the father of John the Baptist, when he wrote his son's name (Luke 1:63).

Papyrus, a term from which our word "paper" is derived, was for many centuries the most common writing material. It was made from the papyrus plant that grew in the delta of the Nile River in Egypt. The center section of the stalk was removed and cut into thin strips that were laid side by side. A second layer was then laid across it to form a sheet ranging in size from 6 by 9 inches to 12 by 15 inches (see Fig. 1). Sheets were normally pasted together

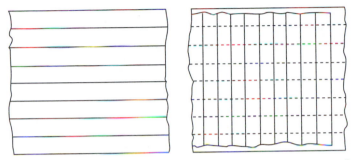

Fig. 1 Papyrus construction, showing the papyrus strips before and after being overlaid.

and sold in rolls of twenty. Writing was usually done on one side only, although occasionally a scroll had writing on both sides (see Rev. 5:1). The autographs of the Greek New Testament were almost certainly written on papyrus. It has been estimated that Paul's shorter letters would have been written on a single papyrus sheet, while the Gospel of Luke would have required a papyrus roll about 30 feet long. In modern times, both biblical and secular papyri have been uncovered in the dry sands of Egypt.

Animal skins, known as vellum or parchment, were also used to receive writing. Once the skins were scraped and dried, they produced a durable and smooth writing surface. By the third or fourth century, parchment was the common writing material in the ancient world, although papyrus continued to be used as late as the seventh century. Practi-

15

cally all surviving manuscripts of the Greek New Testament are written on parchment. Only the very earliest New Testament manuscripts are written on papyrus (see Fig. 2).

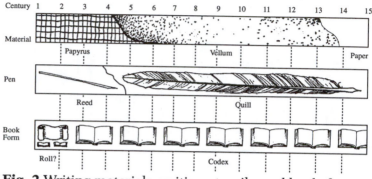

Fig. 2 Writing materials, writing utensils, and book forms.

Because the supply of parchment was limited, when a parchment was no longer wanted the writing was sometimes scraped off and a new text written over it. Such a manuscript was called a "palimpsest" (from πάλιν [*palin*], "again," and ψάω [*psaō*], "I scrape"). Some fifty manuscripts of the Greek New Testament are palimpsests.

Types of Errors in the New Testament Manuscripts

Because textual criticism deals with various kinds of errors found in the existing Greek manuscripts, it is necessary to know something about the types of errors that can occur. The two basic categories of errors are *accidental* and *intentional*. Accidental errors often resulted from the text being read aloud and the scribes relying on their hearing to record it. Romans 5:1 contains a classic example of an error of hearing. Here the slight distinction between long and short vowels in Greek produces a difference in meaning between "we have peace with God" (following the indicative ἔχομεν [echomen], "we have") and "let us have peace with God" (following the subjunctive ἔχωμεν [echōmen], "let us have"). Other types of accidental errors include those stemming from misunderstanding or forgetfulness. The result would be changes in word order, the substitution of synonyms, and the unintentional harmonization of similar passages.

Scribes also made intentional errors. These changes were no doubt made in good faith under the impression that a linguistic or theological error had crept into the text. These "improvements" include changes to correct an apparent error of fact, harmonizations of parallel passages, doctrinal corrections, and improvements in grammar, spelling, and style. Sometimes a scribe believed a marginal notation to be part of the original text and copied it. On other occasions, quotations from the Old Testament were made to agree with their Old Testament forms. Still other deliberate changes were made to round off the meaning of a passage. (For additional examples of errors, see Appendix 1.)

Sources of Evidence for New Testament Textual Criticism

To have a well-rounded picture of the text-critical task, we need to add one other element: the source of evidence for textual criticism. The New Testament textual critic uses three kinds of materials in determining the original text: (1) Greek manuscripts, (2) ancient versions, and (3) citations by early church "fathers" (authoritative writers and teachers of the early centuries). Significantly, in comparison with other ancient documents, the New Testament materials are embarrassingly rich. There are almost five thousand manuscripts of part or all of the Greek New Testament, eight thousand manuscripts in Latin, and a thousand additional manuscripts in other ancient versions. Extensive portions of the New Testament were copied within three centuries after the New Testament books were originally written. Indeed, the materials for recovering the original text of the New Testament are so vast that their study is a somewhat complicated task. Even in the Book of Revelation, which is the most poorly attested writing in the New Testament, over three hundred Greek manuscripts have been preserved.

Let us now take a brief look at these witnesses to the original text of the New Testament.

Greek Manuscripts

The Greek manuscripts have traditionally been divided into four groups: papyri, uncials, minuscules, and lectionaries. The earliest New Testament manuscripts are written on papyrus. Since papyrus was a very fragile writing material, few early copies of the New Testament have survived except in the dry sands of Egypt. Papyrus manuscripts are designated by the letter "p" with a superscript numeral and range in date from approximately A.D. 125 (p^{52}, containing John 18:31–34, 37–38) to the early eighth century. Most papyrus manuscripts of the New Testament date from the third and fourth centuries. Fragments or large sections of approximately eighty-eight papyri are known. Notable groups of papyri include the Chester Beatty papyri from the third century (p^{45}, p^{46}, p^{47}); the Bodmer collection, ranging in date from the late second to the seventh century (p^{66}, p^{72}, p^{73}, p^{74}, p^{75}); and the John Rylands fragment on John 18 (p^{52}). Every New Testament book is attested by at least one papyrus manuscript.

As we have seen, by the fourth century parchment began to replace papyrus as the primary writing material. These early parchment manuscripts are called "uncials," a term that refers to the style of the Greek letters used in writing (which are similar to modern capital letters). Uncial manuscripts date from the fourth to the tenth century and are designated in two ways: by capital letters taken from Hebrew, Latin, and Greek (e.g., A), and by Arabic numerals with a zero prefixed (e.g., 02). Approximately 274 uncials are known today. The most significant of these include Codex Sinaiticus (designated by ℵ [aleph, the first letter of the Hebrew alphabet] or by 01, and dating from the fourth century), Codex Alexandrinus (A, 02, fourth century), Codex Vaticanus (B, 03, fourth century), Codex Ephraemi Rescriptus (C, 04, fourth century), and Codex Bezae (D, 05, late fifth century). Codex Sinaiticus has the distinction of being the earliest surviving *complete* copy of the Greek New Testament. Most uncial manuscripts contain complete books or large sections of the New Testament such as the Gospels. A few of them, such as Codex Vaticanus, originally contained the complete Greek Bible, though parts of these manuscripts are now lost.

In the ninth century a style of writing developed out of the cursive or "running" hand that had been used for private writing. This new style was called "minuscule" ("small lettered"), and it had the great advantage of allowing more rapid writing than the uncial style (see Fig. 3). By the end of the tenth century the minuscule

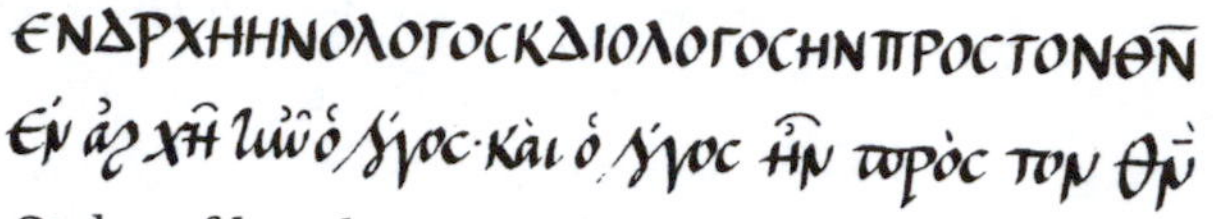

ΕΝΔΡΧΗΗΝΟΛΟΓΟΣΚΔΙΟΛΟΓΟΣΗΝΠΡΟΣΤΟΝΘΝ

Ἐν ἀρχῆ ἰωῦ ὁ λγος· Καὶ ὁ λγος ἦν προς τον θν

Fig. 3 Styles of handwriting, showing the first two clauses of John 1:1 in uncial and minuscule script

style of writing had virtually replaced the uncial. Minuscule manuscripts are designated by Arabic numerals (e.g., 13); approximately 2,555 of these manuscripts are known today. The more significant minuscule manuscripts include Codex 1 (twelfth century), Codex 13 (thirteenth century), and Codex 33 (ninth century). Codex 700 (eleventh century) contains many interesting variations, including the petition in the Lukan version of the Lord's Prayer, "Your Holy Spirit come upon us and cleanse us," instead of, "Your kingdom come." The earlier minuscule manuscripts tend to be more carefully copied than the later ones and to have little or no ornamentation. The vast majority of New Testament Greek manuscripts are minuscules.

The Greek lectionaries are manuscripts containing New Testament passages. These passages are not given in regular sequence but as weekly lessons for reading in the church's worship services. There are about two thousand known lectionary manuscripts of the New

Testament. They are designated by the letter *l* or by the abbreviation *Lect*. All New Testament books except Revelation are excerpted in the lectionaries, though some books (such as Acts) are cited far from completely. The text of most lectionaries is quite similar to that found in the majority of minuscules. A few of the lectionaries are as early as the fifth century (e.g., *l* 1043), but the majority date from the tenth century and later.

The original books of the New Testament were probably written on scrolls. However, because of the need to find specific passages quickly, the scroll form was soon replaced by the codex, or leaf, form. All extant manuscripts of the Greek New Testament are codexes, although some scholars have tried to identify certain Greek fragments of scrolls discovered at Qumran with portions of the New Testament. The codex form allowed Christians to include several documents in a single book, and eventually copies of the entire New Testament were produced.

It is important to understand that the autographs and early copies of the Greek New Testament were written in ancient style. There were no spaces between words, no punctuation marks, and no paragraph divisions. Occasionally the lack of spaces between words could make an important difference. You may recall the story of the atheist who wrote on the chalkboard, "GODISNOWHERE," intending to mean, "God is nowhere." He was quickly corrected by a little girl. "You mean," she said, "God is now here!" Similarly, translators of the earliest copies had to decide where to divide words, where to begin and end sentences, and where to put punctuation. Unfortunately, some of their choices were wrong. First Corinthians 11:1 clearly belongs to the end of chapter 10, and 1 Corinthians 12:31b clearly belongs to the beginning of chapter 13, the great "Love Chapter." Some modern versions translate each verse as a separate paragraph. This can easily confuse the reader who does not realize that the verses were not part of the original text.

As we have seen, the Greek witnesses to the text of the New Testament number around five thousand, ranging between the second and the eighteenth centuries. In comparison, manuscripts of the Hebrew Old Testament number perhaps half as many, though the text of these manuscripts is more uniform than that exhibited by the manuscripts of the New Testament. Moreover, the earliest surviving copies of the New Testament are much closer to the date of the original writing than is the case with almost any other piece of ancient literature. There is even the possibility, or probability, that new discoveries of ancient Greek manuscripts will yet be made. These discoveries will undoubtedly throw additional light on the original words of the New Testament.

Ancient Versions

During the second century the Greek New Testament began to be translated into other languages. The most significant of these early translations (versions) for New Testament textual criticism are the Latin, Syriac, and Coptic.

The New Testament began to be translated into Latin in the second century. The Latin versions include the Old Latin, stemming from North Africa, and the Latin Vulgate, a revision of the Old Latin made by Jerome in A.D. 386. The Vulgate was based on the best available Latin texts, which were compared with some old Greek manuscripts. Subsequently, the Vulgate itself became badly corrupted, so that the eight thousand manuscripts of the Vulgate that have survived are filled with divergent readings. In 1592 Pope Clement VIII prepared a revision of the Vulgate, and the "Clementine" version has been the official Latin Bible of the Roman Catholic Church to the present day. The Syriac versions include the Old Syriac, preserved in two manuscripts, and the Palestinian Syriac, dated to the fifth century. The Coptic includes several dialects, including the Sahidic spoken in Upper (i.e., southern) Egypt, and the Bohairic spoken in Lower (i.e., northern) Egypt. Other versions of the New Testament include the Armenian, Georgian, Ethiopic, Gothic, and Arabic translations.

The importance of these ancient versions for New Testament textual criticism is somewhat limited. None of the original manuscripts of the versions is extant, and therefore existing manuscripts must be subjected to textual criticism to determine the original text as nearly as possible. In addition, in certain types of variants, some versions cannot reflect what the Greek might have read. For instance, Latin lacks the definite article "the," and the Syriac cannot distinguish between the aorist and perfect tenses. However, the great benefit of versional evidence is that it can show that a particular reading was known in the place and time of the version's origin. Thus, for example, a reading supported by the Old Latin would have been known in the West from at least the beginning of the second century.

Citations from the Church Fathers

Citations in the writings of the early church fathers furnish an additional basis for evaluating variants in the Greek New Testament. These writers quoted extensively from the New Testament, using forms of the text known to them. In fact, it has been said that if all the New Testament manuscripts were destroyed, the text of the New Testament could still be restored from the quotations made by the church fathers. Their citations can establish how the text appeared in particular places and during particular periods in church history. For example, we can date the reading "Bethabara" for "Bethany" (John 1:28) to Origen's day (ca. 230), since he could not locate Bethany during his travels in Palestine and suggested the name "Bethabara." As in the case of the versions, however, caution must be noted when using patristic citations. It is often difficult to tell whether a scriptural text is being quoted directly or only being alluded to. Moreover, scribes would sometimes alter the texts of the fathers when copying them. Nevertheless, patristic citations are an important source of information about the New Testament text.

The sheer number of witnesses to the text of the New Testament makes it virtually certain that the original text has been preserved somewhere among the extant witnesses. This means that "conjectural emendation" (the proposal of a reading not found in any surviving witness) should be called upon as a last resort, if at all. This contrasts sharply with Old Testament textual criticism, where conjectural emendation is a frequent necessity.

Conclusion

This chapter began with an appeal for all serious students of the New Testament to engage in textual criticism. It then went on to describe the scope of the text-critical task. Finally, we looked at the sources of evidence available to the New Testament textual critic. The key thoughts of this chapter may be summarized as follows:

- The goal of textual criticism is to search with great care and diligence for that reading which is closest to the autographs.
- Textual criticism is a necessary, if also a demanding, field of study. *Interpretation and textual criticism are inseparably related.*
- No biblical doctrine would go unsupported if a favorite reading was abandoned in favor of a more valid variant. This does not mean, as is sometimes said, that no doctrine of Scripture is affected by textual variation. Rather, a doctrine that is affected by textual variation will always be adequately supported by other passages.
- Textual errors may either be intentional or unintentional, though it is not always possible to tell one kind of error from the other.
- Our knowledge of the New Testament text is derived from three principal sources: Greek manuscripts, early versions, and patristic citations.
- Textual criticism needs to operate in only a limited, albeit important, portion of the text. Just

how textual criticism does this is the subject of our next chapter.

Questions for Discussion

1. Chapter and verse divisions were added to our Bibles a few hundred years ago. Do these divisions make a difference in the way you understand your New Testament? Can you cite any examples?

2. If you understand something about how textual variants arose, how will it make a difference in the way you interpret the Bible?

3. To consider questions of textual variation, scan the Book of Romans in an English version that contains marginal notes (e.g., the NASB, NKJV, or NRSV). Make a list of all the different variant readings that occur in the book. Do you think an understanding of these variants is important for your understanding of the message of Romans?

2

From Corruption to Restoration

The History and Methods of New Testament Textual Criticism

Introduction

In the previous chapter we considered the purpose and materials of New Testament textual criticism. Now we must go on to consider the procedure of textual criticism. However, in order to understand the various modern approaches to New Testament textual criticism, a sketch of the history of the subject is necessary.

The History of New Testament Textual Criticism

The Earliest Centuries

In the first three centuries after the Greek New Testament was written, the text of the New Testament developed rather freely. Scribes would make copies from other copies, and soon manuscripts began to take on textual peculiarities of other manuscripts. For example, in the Lord's Prayer (Matt. 6:13), some manuscripts contain the words "For yours is the kingdom and the power and the glory forever. Amen," while other manuscripts do not. In some manuscripts of Matthew 5:22, Jesus condemns the person who is angry "without a cause," while in other manuscripts the prohibition is total. While numerous manuscripts of Ephesians contain the words "in Ephesus" in 1:1, a few omit them. Some manuscripts of John 1:18 read "the only Son," while others read "the only God." Manuscripts containing these and other variants soon arose in various locales, giving rise to the creation of manuscript families, or "text types." Today, these manuscript families are known as the "Alexandrian," "Western," and "Byzantine" text types. This classification into families is based upon agreement of a group of manuscripts in a large number of variant readings. For example, if a group of manuscripts exhibits fifty or one hundred common readings that are found nowhere else, it can be concluded that these variants stem from a common source. Eventually the New Testament writings were given canonical status, and scribes had less freedom to change the text. This means that most variants probably arose before the end of the third century.

The Middle Ages and Beyond

By the seventh century the use of Greek had all but disappeared, except in the Byzantine empire. Hence, by the time the printing press was invented, the Byzantine text type used by the Greek Orthodox Church was the dominant form of the Greek text.

The first Greek New Testament to be printed was produced in Spain in 1514, but it was not issued until 1522. It was part of a polyglot (multilanguage) Bible edited by Cardinal Ximenes of Toledo. Meanwhile, the famous humanist scholar Erasmus of Rotterdam was hastily preparing an edition of the Greek New Testament under the patronage of the Swiss printer Froben. Erasmus's New Testament was printed in Basel in 1516 after only six months of preparation. This was one year before Luther delivered his theses in Wittenberg, and it provided the Greek basis from which Luther later translated the New Testament into German (1522). The third edition of Erasmus appeared in 1522 and was used for Tyndale's translation in 1525, the language of which is still embedded in the King James Version.

The text of Erasmus was based on the few late Byzantine manuscripts that were available to him, and he had to supply missing portions of the Book of Revelation. The same basic text was later published by the Paris printer Robert Estienne (Stephanus) and by the Elziver brothers of Holland. The preface to the latters' 1633 edition contained the famous words: "Textum ergo habes, nunc ab omnibus receptum" ("You have therefore the text now received by all"). From this statement arose the designation *Textus Receptus*, or the "Received Text" (often referred to as the "TR"). This is the text underlying the King James Version of 1611,

29

and was the main Greek text until the publication of the English Revised Version in 1881.

The Modern Era

A significant number of ancient manuscripts of the New Testament (and of the Old Testament in Greek) were brought to light between the sixteenth and nineteenth centuries. These manuscripts were from an earlier period than those used by Erasmus. Because they were older, they were considered by many scholars to be closer to the autographs. Moreover, as the manuscripts were studied, it became clear that they differed in numerous places from the texts that had been previously used.

Building on the work of such textual critics as Griesbach and Lachmann, the great Cambridge scholars B. F. Westcott and F. J. A. Hort inaugurated a new era in New Testament textual criticism with the publication in 1881 of their *New Testament in the Original Greek*. This edition of the Greek New Testament became widely accepted as the standard text. It was accompanied by a volume carefully explaining the principles upon which their work was based. The Westcott and Hort text was derived from manuscripts that differed considerably from those used by Erasmus. Westcott and Hort argued that the Byzantine text (which they called the "Syrian text") had been officially edited by the fourth-century church, and that its readings were inferior to those found in the best Alexandrian manuscripts. This left them with three text types: the Western, the Alexandrian, and a group closely akin to the Alexandrian, which they called the "Neutral text" because they thought it to be free from contamination. The Neutral text included Codexes Sinaiticus and Vaticanus.

Believing sincerely that they were improving the New Testament text, Westcott and Hort rejected a number of familiar readings in preference for what they thought were more accurate readings. Since 1881 the majority of English translations of the New Testament—including the New American Standard Bible, the New International Version, the Revised English Bible, and the New Revised Standard Version—have used a text that is much closer to the one published by Westcott and Hort than the one issued by Erasmus. The main exception to this is the New King James Version, which is based on the Textus Receptus. Major differences between the Textus Receptus and a modern critical text include the following: (1) the omission or addition of substantial passages (Matt. 16:2b, 3; Mark 16:9–20; Luke 22:19b, 20, 43, 44; John 7:53–8:11; 1 John 5:7, 8); (2) the omission or addition of shorter passages (Matt. 6:13; 17:21; 18:11; 21:44; Mark 9:44, 46; Luke 9:56; Acts 8:37; Rom. 16:24); (3) the substitution of a word (or words) for another (1 Tim. 3:16; Rev. 22:14); and (4) the omission or addition of a single word or group of words (Matt. 6:4, 6; 1 Cor. 6:20; 11:24; 1 John 3:1).

In the twentieth century the New Testament in Greek has been edited by both Protestant and Roman Catholic scholars. The most widely used forms of the text are the Nestle-Aland *Novum Testamentum Graece* (26th ed.) and the United Bible Societies' *Greek New Testament* (4th ed.). Other scholars, arguing that the text underlying the King James Version is closest to the originals, have edited *The Greek New Testament According to the Majority Text* (1982). The differences between these various Greek texts are often significant, and can be seen in the marginal notes provided in the standard English translations.

Principles for Establishing the Original Reading

As we have seen, textual criticism has developed certain principles for establishing original readings based on both external and internal criteria. These principles cannot be thoughtlessly applied, nor do all apply in each instance of textual variation. Nevertheless, familiarity with the basic principles will increase one's ability to resolve a textual problem when it is encountered in reading or exegesis.

Principles of External Evidence

External evidence seeks to determine which reading is supported by the most reliable witnesses (Greek manuscripts, versions, and patristic citations). Most of these witnesses can be loosely grouped into one of three basic families or text types according to variant readings that occur in them.

The *Alexandrian text* (so named because of its apparent emergence in and around Alexandria, Egypt) is represented by the majority of papyri, several early uncials (e.g., ℵ, B, C), the Coptic versions, and important Alexandrian fathers (e.g., Clement, Origen). It is characterized by readings that are generally shorter and more difficult, and by refined grammatical corrections. Although many modern scholars prefer the Alexandrian text type, others have questioned its readings, especially where it stands alone. Moreover, the tendency among some scholars (mostly German) to regard this text type as a new "Standard Text" has not been well received in certain quarters. It should also be noted that new discoveries (especially the papyri) have led contemporary textual critics to lay aside Westcott and Hort's Neutral text. In practical terms, this means that at any given point even the oldest manuscripts (such as א and B) may be wrong.

The so-called *Western text* is represented by the uncial D, the Old Latin, the Old Syriac, and a few other witnesses (Irenaeus, Tertullian, Jerome). Generally speaking, it is characterized by harmonistic tendencies and additions (e.g., the Western text of Acts is about 8 percent longer than the Alexandrian text of the same book). Scholars continue to debate both the origin and value of the Western text, and most are hesitant to accept readings that contain only Western support.

The *Byzantine text* is represented by the vast majority of Greek manuscripts and most of the later church fathers. This text was largely preserved in the area of the old Byzantine empire, which is now Turkey, Bulgaria, Greece, Albania, and the former Yugoslavia. Because of the influence of Westcott and Hort, the Byzantine text is now considered to be the least valuable text type. Its readings are described as smooth and unobjectionable, and difficult readings appear to have been alleviated. Some scholars, however, continue to champion this text type as the one closest to the original, and even those scholars who prefer the Alexandrian text would be reluctant to reject a Byzantine reading automatically. In fact, distinctively Byzantine readings can be found in very ancient witnesses and may almost certainly be original.

Scholars occasionally refer to a fourth text type—the Caesarean. Found only in the Gospels, this group of manuscripts is often found in company with the Alexandrian or Western text types. Today, however, there is little consensus as to the existence of this group of witnesses. It appears to be the most mixed of any of the groups that can be classified as a text type.

Employing these various witnesses to the New Testament text, scholars have developed certain principles (or "canons") of external evidence. These principles include the following.

(1) *Prefer the reading attested by the oldest manuscripts.* Generally speaking, earlier manuscripts are more important than later ones for establishing the text. This principle must be used with caution, however, since an early manuscript may exhibit a corrupted text, while a later copy may reflect a more reliable form of the text. For example, manuscript 1739 (tenth century) preserves a text closely related to p^{46} (ca. 200). Therefore, it is often necessary to distinguish between the date of a *manuscript* and the date of its *readings*, the date of the reading being the important thing. It is also vital to remember that even the oldest Greek manuscripts have undergone editing like all other manuscripts. This raises serious questions about the blind preference some editors and commentators show for particular manuscripts.

(2) *Prefer the reading supported in widely separated geographical areas.* Other things being equal, a geographically widespread reading is more likely to be original than a reading preserved in only one locale. A reading, for example, with support from Rome, Asia Minor, Caesarea, and North Africa is more likely to be original than one supported only by Alexandrian witnesses.

(3) *Prefer the reading supported by the greatest number of text types.* A consensus of witnesses—manuscripts, versions, and fathers—is necessary before we can say that a *text type* supports a particular reading. The important principle to remember is: *the greater number of text types in support of a reading, the greater probability of its originality.*

Principles of Internal Evidence

Internal evidence involves both *transcriptional probabilities* (having to do with the habits and practices of scribes) and *intrinsic probabilities* (having to do with the author's style and vocabulary). But the basic principle of internal evidence is: *the reading that best explains the origin of the other readings is probably original.* This principle has several corollaries.

(1) *Prefer the shorter reading,* since scribes more often added to the text than omitted words. However, this principle must be used cautiously, since scribes sometimes omitted material either accidentally or because they found something to be grammatically, stylistically, or theologically objectionable in the text.

(2) *Prefer the more difficult reading,* since scribes usually altered a difficult text to make it easier

rather than vice versa.

(3) *Prefer the reading that accords best with the author's style and vocabulary.* Words or phrases that are clearly out of harmony with an author's writing habits or diction are generally suspect if a variant is involved.

(4) *Prefer the reading that best fits the context and/or the author's theology.* Here exegesis of the entire passage is crucial for the text-critical question.

(5) *Prefer the less harmonious reading in parallel passages.* The tendency of scribes was to make parallel texts conform with each other (cf. the Matthean and Lukan forms of the Lord's Prayer).

Of course, the greatest caution must be exercised in applying these principles. They are inferences rather than axiomatic rules. Indeed, it is not uncommon for two or more principles to conflict. Hence none of them can be applied in a mechanical or unthinking fashion. If in the end you are still undecided, you should pay special attention to external evidence, as it is less subjective and more reliable.

Modern Approaches to New Testament Textual Criticism

Not all scholars consider the above principles equally valid or applicable to New Testament textual criticism. Today, four approaches to textual criticism can be seen among New Testament scholars. Each of the four current approaches may be identified with individual scholars. For the sake of convenience, these approaches may be called Radical Eclecticism, Reasoned Eclecticism, Reasoned Conservatism, and Radical Conservatism. The term "eclectic" means that the scholar tends to view each textual variant on its own merits instead of blindly following one manuscript or group of manuscripts. The term "conservative" is used here to refer to a generally high view of the traditional Byzantine text type and/or the Textus Receptus.

Radical Eclecticism (G. D. Kilpatrick, J. K. Elliott)

Radical Eclecticism holds to what may be called a purely eclectic text. This approach prefers a text based solely on internal evidence. Adherents of this view argue that since the history of the New Testament text is untraceable, none of the text types carries any weight. Hence the reading of *any* manuscript may be original, since no manuscript or group of manuscripts is "best." An eclectic scholar will thus choose the reading that commends itself as best fitting the context, whether in style or thought. This view, held primarily by a minority of British scholars, has been criticized for ignoring the value and importance of the external evidence, particularly the Greek manuscripts.

Reasoned Eclecticism (B. M. Metzger, K. Aland)

Reasoned Eclecticism holds that the text of the New Testament is to be based on both internal and external evidence, without a preference for any particular manuscript or text type. This view of the text is represented in the Nestle-Aland and United Bible Societies' Greek New Testaments. This approach often represents a predilection for manuscripts of the Alexandrian text type. This preference is based largely on Westcott and Hort's theory that the Byzantine text is a conflation of the Alexandrian and Western texts, and that the superiority of the Alexandrian text over the Western text can be shown through internal evidence. This approach has occasionally been criticized for producing a new "Textus Receptus"—a canonized form of the New Testament text.

Reasoned Conservatism (H. A. Sturz)

What might be called Reasoned Conservatism holds that each of the main text types is equally early and independent, going back separately into the second century. Like Reasoned Eclecticism, Reasoned Conservatism sees both internal and external evidence as useful. However, unlike Reasoned Eclecticism, which tends to follow the Alexandrian text, Reasoned Conservatism insists that no single text type can be preferred over all others, and instead emphasizes the geographical distribution of the text types. Scholars who hold to this view argue that the Byzantine text is older than the age of the earliest Byzantine manuscript (fifth century). For example, Byzantine readings once thought to be late have been found in early Egyptian papyri. Therefore, adherents of this view consider the Byzantine text type to be an early and independent witness to the text of the New Testament. They further believe that the reading that is the consensus of the majority of text types is most representative of the autographs. Reasoned Conservatism has been criticized for restoring the Byzantine text (which many feel to be "corrupt") to a place of usefulness.

Radical Conservatism (Z. Hodges, A. Farstad)

Finally, the approach that may be called Radical Conservatism holds that the Byzantine text type most closely approximates the original text of the New Testament. Scholars who hold to this view prefer the reading of the majority of manuscripts, which are, of course, mainly Byzantine. Several of these scholars have produced the New King James Version, which is based on the Textus Receptus, thus perpetuating the tradition begun by William Tyndale in 1525 and continued in the King James Version of 1611. This approach has been criticized for being too mechanical and for ignoring the fact that manuscripts must be weighed and not just counted. For example, if ten manuscripts are copies of a single parent manuscript, then an error appearing in the parent will appear ten times in ten copies. But these ten copies are equal to a single authority, not to ten.

These four approaches to New Testament textual criticism may be summarized as follows:

1. Radical Eclecticism
   a. The text is to be based on internal evidence alone.
   b. No manuscript or group of manuscripts is to be preferred.
   c. The result is a purely "eclectic" text.
2. Reasoned Eclecticism
   a. The text is to be based on both internal and external evidence.

      b. The reading of the "best" manuscripts is generally to be preferred.

      c. The result is a "critical" text.

  3. Reasoned Conservatism

      a. The text is to be based on both internal and external evidence.

      b. The reading of the majority of text types is to be preferred.

      c. The result is a "widespread" text.

  4. Radical Conservatism.

      a. The text is to be based on external evidence alone.

      b. The reading of the majority of manuscripts is to be preferred.

      c. The result is a "majority" text.

Even though these various schools of thought can be identified, it is necessary to realize that textual critics might partially adopt the approaches of two or more schools, so that a synthesis often results. Likewise, schools tend to fluctuate over time due to the influx of new leaders and materials.

Conclusion

Our purpose in this chapter has been to paint a picture of the text-critical task in broad strokes. If you have received a general impression of that task, this will suffice for now. Almost everything covered in this chapter will be illustrated in greater detail in Chapter 3.

One thing, however, should be clear: the study of New Testament textual criticism is a never-ending task. Much work remains to be done before anything approaching a consensus can be reached. Perhaps the most significant question concerns the nature of the Byzantine text type. Does this text represent a revision made in Antioch in the fourth century, as Westcott and Hort believed? There is little historical data to support this view, and most modern scholars who argue that Byzantine manuscripts are secondary do so on the basis of internal evidence. At the very least, it must be conceded that (1) no single text type is infallible or to be preferred because of its supposed superior authority; (2) each reading must be examined on its own merits; and (3) readings that best explain other variants merit our preference. In short, since no hypothesis thus far proposed to explain the history of the text has gained general assent, in order to arrive at the original text the critic must compare readings on a case by case basis, and in each case select the reading that commends itself in the light of both external and internal evidence.

Questions for Discussion

1. Using a copy of the King James Version (or the New King James Version) and at least one modern version based on the "critical" text (e.g., the New American Standard Bible, the New International Version, or the New Revised Standard Version), compare the variants listed above on page 31. How would these variants affect your interpretation of the New Testament?
2. Which of the four approaches to New Testament textual criticism discussed in this chapter seems the most valid? What are the strengths and weaknesses of each?

3

From Theory to Practice

Selected Examples of New Testament Textual Criticism

Introduction

In the preceding chapter, we briefly outlined the criteria for doing New Testament textual criticism. In this chapter we will attempt to apply these criteria by analyzing several examples of variation. I will be shamelessly neutral in my presentation. In the recent past, a portion of the academic world has become an arena for a genteel battle between theorists; but for our purposes we will adopt the best that each approach has to offer, and consider how each might offset the weaknesses of the other. This is an ecumenical age, and there is no reason why we cannot achieve some kind of synthesis that is pertinent to our primary object—the better understanding of the New Testament.

How to Read a Textual Apparatus

Before starting, however, we need to become familiar with the critical apparatuses of the most commonly used editions of the Greek New Testament. Most students will have either the United Bible Societies' *Greek New Testament* or the Nestle-Aland *Novum Testamentum Graece.* Of course, neither of these editions covers all of the available manuscripts, versions, and patristic citations. Instead, representatives of larger groups of witnesses are given. This is the best that a handy edition of the Greek New Testament can do.

The United Bible Societies' Greek New Testament

The apparatus provided in the *Greek New Testament* is fairly simple. It is separated from the main text by a solid black line that runs across the entire page. Each set of notes is numbered, beginning with "1." This is followed by a boldface numeral that corresponds with the verse number in the text where the variant under discussion is found. The verse number is then followed by a bracket containing the letters A, B, C, or D. These letters indicate the relative certainty of the reading printed in the text ("A" indicates virtual certainty, "B" only some degree of doubt, "C" a considerable degree of doubt, "D" a very high degree of doubt). Following immediately is the reading that was adopted by the editorial committee and printed in the text. The manuscript support that follows is listed in the following order: papyrus manuscripts, uncials, minuscules, lectionaries, versions, and fathers. Then comes the reading(s) rejected by the committee, preceded by a pair of vertical lines. For the other symbols used in the apparatus, consult the introduction to the *Greek New Testament*.

The Nestle-Aland Novum Testamentum Graece

This apparatus is considerably more complicated than that found in the United Bible Societies' *Greek New Testament*, and it also contains many more variants (the ratio is about 5:1). The coverage of manuscripts is less full, and usually only those readings not adopted in the text are cited. It uses symbols for the four major types of variants in the New Testament: additions, omissions, substitutions, and transpositions. A list of these symbols appears in the introduction to the text (which should be read). Since generally there are several variants listed for each verse, a black dot is used to set off additional variants in the same verse. The Nestle-Aland edition of the Greek New Testament is preferred by scholars and serious students because it affords a glimpse at more variants and because the reader can easily identify the types of variants involved simply by noting the symbols used in the text.

Examples of New Testament Textual Criticism

The best way of learning about textual criticism is by working through a number of examples. For the most part, the variants discussed below are those I have had an opportunity to treat in greater detail elsewhere (see the Select Bibliography). Since it can be assumed that you are familiar with the rudiments of New Testament Greek, it is recommended that you have your Greek New Testament handy when working through the following examples.

Mark 1:2

Our first example is fairly cut-and-dried. In Mark 1:2 the manuscripts offer the following possibilities: (1) "as it is written in Isaiah the prophet"; (2) "as it is written in the prophets." There are two reasons for preferring the former reading. First, the manuscript evidence for reading (1) is both early and widespread (ℵ, B, D, L, Θ, 33, Old Latin, Vulgate), while the evidence for reading (2) is limited to the Byzantine text type (A, K, P, W, *Byz*). As we have seen, the more geographically widespread reading is generally to be preferred. Second, the internal evidence clearly supports reading (1). Reading (2) doubtless arose because the quotations that follow are not only from Isaiah but include one from Malachi as well. By the change from "in Isaiah the prophet" to "in the prophets," this apparent discrepancy was alleviated. Thus both lines of evidence—external and internal—combine in support of variant (1).

Matthew 5:22

Our second example is found in Matthew 5:22 and is a bit more problematic. Did Jesus forbid all anger or only anger "without a cause" (εἰκῇ [*eikē*])? The variants are the following: (1) "Everyone who is angry with his brother is liable to judgment"; (2) "Everyone who is angry with his brother without a cause [εἰκῇ] is liable to judgment."

The internal evidence allows for two possibilities. In the first place, one could argue that the word εἰκῇ was added to soften Jesus' statement. This was the opinion of the committee that edited the *Greek New Testament* (see Metzger's *Textual Commentary*, p. 13): "Although the reading with εἰκῇ is widespread from the second century onwards, it is much more likely that the word was added by copyists in order to soften the rigor of the precept, than omitted as unnecessary." In other words, a scribe, thinking that Jesus was being too rigid, inserted the word εἰκῇ to soften his statement.

The internal evidence may, however, be understood in the opposite way, for Jesus may have wanted to qualify his teaching about anger by adding "without a cause." Later, a scribe may have omitted εἰκῇ from his copy because he thought it made Jesus appear too indulgent to anger. Hence the internal evidence, as so often the case, is inconclusive. Internal considerations frequently cancel each other out or are indecisive.

Looking now at the external evidence, we see that the shorter text has impressive support (p[67], ℵ, B, Vulgate). However, it competes with a reading that is equally early and yet more widespread in its attestation. Behind the reading εἰκῇ are the Western (D, Old Latin) and Byzantine (K, W, and many others) text types, as well as Alexandrian witnesses (L, Coptic). On the other hand, the omission of εἰκῇ is supported almost exclusively by Alexandrian witnesses. Thus in terms of geographical distribution, the support for the longer reading is overwhelming. In short, although both readings are equally early, external criteria argue that εἰκῇ, as the more widespread reading, is to be preferred over its more limited alternative.

Ephesians 1:1

Our third example comes from Ephesians 1:1. Are the words "in Ephesus" (ἐν Ἐφέσῳ [en Phesō]) original or not? Here the external evidence seems to favor the inclusion of the words. The longer reading is both early and widespread, being supported by the great majority of Greek manuscripts (A, D, G, K, P, 33, *Byz*), ancient versions (Old Latin, Vulgate, Syriac, Coptic), and church fathers (Ambrosiaster, Chrysostom, Cyril, Theodoret), as well as by the majority of text types (the Western and the Byzantine). On the other hand, the testimony for the omission of "in Ephesus" is extremely limited (p[46], ℵ, B, Origen).

If, however, the words "in Ephesus" were original, why would anyone want to omit them? The usual reasons for accidental omission do not seem to apply in this case. A remote possibility is that the name "Ephesus" was abbreviated and somehow in its shortened form overlooked by a careless scribe. No evidence exists, however, that Christian scribes ever accepted into their system of contractions the names of cities.

Perhaps the most plausible explanation is that the address was omitted in order to make the letter a "catholic" (i.e., universal) epistle, intended for the church at large rather than for a specific congregation. Recent scholarship has shown that the early church struggled with the "peculiarity" of the Pauline epistles. The issue was: How can we read a letter as applicable to our situation when that letter was originally written for another church? The easiest way to resolve this problem was to omit any reference to a place name in the opening greeting. The same phenomenon can be seen in Romans 1:7, 15, where the words "in Rome" are omitted in a number of manuscripts. Later, when the Pauline letters came to be regarded as Scripture to be read and used by all, this somewhat mechanical way of resolving the problem disappeared.

John 3:13

Our final textual problem is found in John 3:13. Since this variant has important doctrinal implications, it will require a more detailed treatment. The NIV renders the verse as follows: "No one has ever gone into heaven except the one who came from heaven—the Son of Man." The margin indicates that some manuscripts add "who is in heaven" after the words "the Son of Man." This is, in fact, the reading of the NKJV: "No one has ascended to heaven but He who came down from heaven, *that is*, the Son of Man who is in heaven." This is clearly an important variant with significance for New Testament Christology. Did Jesus claim to be present in heaven while he was on earth talking to Nicodemus?

The external evidence may be summarized as follows:

Witnesses to the Text of John 3:13

Reading	Byzantine	Alexandrian	Western	Other ("Caesarean"
(1) ὁ ὢν ἐν τῷ οὐρανῷ "who is in heaven"	A E F G H K M S V Γ Λ Π *Byz Lect* Basil Chrysostom Didymus Nonnus Theodoret	892 Coptic (mss. of the Bohairic) Dionysius Origen	Old Latin Vulgate Syriac (Harclean) Hippolytus Novatian Hillary	Θ f¹ f¹³ 28 565 Armenian Georgian
(2) Omit		p⁶⁶,⁷⁵ ℵ B L 33 Coptic (mss. of the Sahidic; Bohairic) Ethiopic Origen Didymus		
(3) ὃς ἦν ἐν τῷ οὐρανῷ "who was in heaven "			Old Latin (ms. e) Syriac (Curetonian)	
(4) ὁ ὢν ἐκ τοῦ οὐρανοῦ "who is from heaven"			0141 80 Syriac (Sinaitic)	

In assessing this evidence, the following observations can be made. In the first place, the external evidence clearly demonstrates that readings (3) and (4) are secondary. The former has only versional evidence in support, while the latter is supported by only two Greek manuscripts and the Sinaitic Syriac. Each of these readings is an apparent attempt to avoid suggesting that Jesus was on earth and in heaven at the same time.

Variant reading (2)—the omission of "who is in heaven"—is also supported by a relatively small number of manuscripts (p⁶⁶,⁷⁵, ℵ, B) of a single text type (the Alexandrian). However, other Alexandrian witnesses, most notably manuscripts of the Bohairic dialect, indicate that the words ὁ ὢν ἐν τῷ οὐρανῷ were also known early in Egypt.

Finally, the evidence for reading (1) is as follows. The phrase ὁ ὢν ἐν τῷ οὐρανῷ is found in nearly all the uncial and minuscule manuscripts extant in this portion of the New Testament (A, E, F, G, K, Θ, Π, 28, 565) as well as in nearly every ancient version (Old Latin, Vulgate, Armenian, Georgian), including several Bohairic manuscripts from Egypt. Support for the longer reading is also found in the great majority of patristic witnesses, including the Alexandrian father Origen, whose testimony is divided equally between readings (1) and (2). Moreover, the longer reading is not limited to manuscripts of only one geographical area, as is its omission. The words "who is in heaven" were accepted as genuine over a wide geographical area, encompassing most of the then-known ancient world: Rome and the West, Greece, Syria, Palestine, and even Alexandria, the literary capital of Egypt.

These considerations are significant in light of the canons of textual criticism that apply to external evidence. Any reading supported by one text type exclusively is automatically suspect, since no manuscript or text type is perfectly trustworthy. Conversely, a reading supported by two or more text types is to be preferred to a reading supported by only one text type. The external evidence shows almost the entire ancient tradition supporting the longer reading, including the Old Latin, which establishes the date of the longer reading as at least the last quarter of the second century. The testimony of the Greek manuscripts, ancient versions, and church fathers thus forms, as it were, a strong three-cord strand that is not easily broken.

The retreat at this point by many scholars to the early uncials ℵ and B is understandable. The readings of these two manuscripts have long been accepted as original in places of variation. However, despite the acknowledged antiquity and worth of these great uncials, it has become increasingly common since the days of Westcott and Hort to question the readings of these witnesses when they stand alone. This means that the readings of ℵ and B, even when supported by early papyri, cannot be accepted blindly, for the idea of Hort's "Neutral" text is untenable. In fact, there are numerous places where the earliest Alexandrian manuscripts agree in error (see, e.g., John 5:17, 44; 10:18; 13:22; 19:39; 1 Cor. 1:8; 2:10).

Summarizing the external evidence, then, it appears that the most likely original reading is the one that includes the words ὁ ὢν ἐν τῷ οὐρανῷ. The omission, though early and supported by the chief representatives of the Alexandrian text type, is less likely to be authentic due to the scarcity and geographical limitation of manuscript support.

But what about the internal evidence? Let us examine the criteria introduced in Chapter 2.

Prefer the More Difficult Reading

Preference for reading (1) finds strong support from this principle, since the longer reading is obviously the more difficult. It has Christ saying that he was present both in heaven and on earth while talking with Nicodemus. The awkwardness of this saying could easily explain the omission of the words "who is in heaven" as well as the origin of the two other variants in this verse: "who *was* in heaven" (ὃς ἦν ἐν τῷ οὐρανῷ) and "who is *from* heaven" (ὁ ὢν ἐκ τοῦ οὐρανοῦ). Each of these readings can easily be explained as attempts to alleviate the more difficult reading "who *is* in heaven."

Prefer the Shorter Reading

Because scribes were more prone to add words than to omit them, the shorter reading is generally to be preferred. This fact, coupled with the assumed quality of ℵ and B, was no doubt critical in the decision by the editors of the Greek New Testament to relegate the words "who is in heaven" to the apparatus. However, this principle states that the shorter reading is to be preferred *unless* the scribe either accidentally omitted material or else intentionally omitted material on stylistic, grammatical, or doctrinal grounds. Hence it is possible that the words "who is in heaven" were found theologically objectionable (perhaps by a less orthodox scribe) and omitted on that basis. In view of this possibility, the longer reading deserves serious consideration as being original even on the basis of this principle of internal evidence.

Prefer the Reading That Best Accounts for the Others

Had the readings "who was in heaven" or "who is from heaven" been original, there is no reason why a scribe would have altered the text. If, however, the reading "who is in heaven" is original, one can easily understand the other variants as attempts to modify or (in the case of the shorter text) to remove altogether a difficult expression.

There now remains the matter of what the author was more likely to have written. In this regard we must take into account (1) a reading's harmony with the author's teaching elsewhere, and (2) a reading's harmony with the author's style and vocabulary.

The Author's Theology

The longer reading undoubtedly represents a high Christology. Did the author of the Fourth Gospel share such a view? The answer is plain: the Johannine Jesus is not only the preexistent Word (1:1) and the post-resurrection Lord (20:28), but also the Revealer who remained "with God" (1:1) while present on earth (1:14). John's Jesus did not cease to be what he was before the incarnation, for the flesh assumed by the Word was the "tabernacle" in which God was pleased to dwell (1:14). Thus the words "who is in heaven" fit perfectly into the pattern of Johannine Christology.

The Author's Style and Vocabulary

A general knowledge of an author's style and vocabulary often will help determine whether a particular reading is in harmony with the rest of the author's writings. In this instance, a quick check of a Greek concordance reveals that the clause "who is in heaven" faithfully reflects John's characteristic style and vocabulary. Six of the eleven occurrences of the participle "who is" with a prepositional phrase appear in the Fourth Gospel (see 1:18; 3:31; 6:46; 8:47; 12:17; 18:37). Elsewhere, the construction appears only in Matthew 12:30; Luke

11:23; Romans 9:5; 2 Corinthians 11:31; and Ephesians 2:4. Thus, the reading "who is in heaven" is not only Johannine *but almost exclusively* so in the New Testament. Hence there is no linguistic evidence why John could not have written these words.

In summary, although much can be said for certain arguments in favor of the omission of the words "who is in heaven" in John 3:13, the inclusion of the words appears to be the best solution. It is supported by significant external and internal evidence and retains a great deal of John's original use of the term "Son of Man." Hence this witness to Christ's deity, on our reading of the evidence, is not a mere dogma handed down by the church, but a witness deriving from Jesus himself and verified by the apostle John.

The preceding examples should serve to illustrate the principles discussed in the previous chapter, demonstrate that no one manuscript or text type is to be given automatic preference, and make clear that no single canon of textual criticism can be applied in a mechanical or thoughtless fashion.

Dealing with Textual Problems in Preaching and Teaching

A final matter of significance concerns the issue of how to deal with variant readings from the pulpit or podium. Anyone who preaches or teaches from the New Testament regularly will need to know something about textual criticism. As we have seen, the Byzantine text served as the basis for the King James Version, but almost every other translation uses a more modern, "critical" text. Differences between versions could become a divisive issue in one's teaching ministry.

Here are a few suggestions on what to do—and avoid—when dealing with textual variants. In the first place, it is good to keep the discussion short and to the point, remembering that most lay people have no knowledge of Greek at all. Second, help people see that most variants are insignificant, and that no doctrine of Scripture ultimately rests on a disputed passage. Third, be sure to consult Metzger's *Textual Commentary* and other commentaries before expressing an opinion on a place of textual variation. Finally, be careful not to undermine the reliability of the English translations that are being used by your congregation.

Conclusion

Textual criticism is an intricate and demanding field of study, but it is not an impossible field, even for beginners. In this book we have attempted to survey the principal materials and methods of this discipline. As you become increasingly familiar with these matters, your proficiency in resolving textual problems will increase. We may never get to the point where we can guarantee that our interpretation is the only correct one; but we should never get to the point where we should quit trying to understand the original text. Let us take to heart the saying of a great preacher of an earlier generation: "Work as though everything depends upon you; pray as though everything depends upon God."

For Practice

The following passages contain significant textual variations. If you would like to try your hand at resolving one of them on your own, Appendix 3 provides a worksheet for your convenience.

Matt. 6:13	Rom. 5:1
Matt. 17:21	1 Cor. 2:1
Mark 1:1	Phil. 3:3
Mark 16:9–20	1 Thess. 2:7
Luke 4:4	1 Tim. 3:16
John 1:18	James 2:20
John 7:53–8:11	1 John 2:20
	Rev. 1:5

Appendix 1

Types of Errors in the New Testament Manuscripts

Errors occurring in the manuscripts of the Greek New Testament fall into two categories: accidental and intentional. The most frequently encountered errors of these kinds are listed below.

I. **Accidental Errors**
   A. Faulty Word Division
      Example. 1 Timothy 3:16: ὁμολογοῦμεν ὡς μέγα ("we acknowledge how great") for ὁμολογουμένως μέγα ("confessedly great").
   B. Homoeoteleuton ("similar ending")—skipping from one letter or word to the same letter or word farther down the page.

Example. 1 John 2:23: here many manuscripts skip from the first occurrence of τὸν πατέρα ἔχει to the second.
C. Haplography ("single writing")—writing a letter or word once when it should be written twice.
Example. 1 Thessalonians 2:7: ἐγενήθημεν ἤπιοι ("we became gentle") for ἐγενήθημεν νήπιοι ("we became infants").
D. Dittography ("double writing")—writing a letter or word twice instead of once.
Example. Mark 12:27: ὁ θεὸς θεὸς for θεὸς.
E. Metathesis ("change of place")—changing the order of letters or words.
Example. Mark 14:65: ἔλαβον ("received") for ἔβαλον ("struck").
F. Itacism—confusing vowel sounds.
Example. Romans 5:1: ἔχωμεν ("let us have") for ἔχομεν ("we have").
II. **Intentional Errors**
A. Grammatical Improvements
Example. Mark 6:29: ἦλθον for ἦλθαν.
B. Liturgical Changes
Example. Matthew 6:13: addition/omission of the doxology in the Lord's Prayer.
C. Elimination of Apparent Discrepancies
Example. Mark 1:2: ἐν τοῖς προφήταις ("in the prophets") for ἐν τῷ Ἡσαίᾳ τῷ προφήτῃ ("in Isaiah the prophet").
D. Harmonization of Parallel Passages
Example. Matthew 19:17 (cf. Mark 10:18).
E. Conflation—combining two or more variants into one reading.

Example. Luke 24:53: αἰνοῦντες and εὐλογοῦντες may have been conflated to produce the reading αἰνοῦντες καὶ εὐλογοῦντες (though it is also possible that homoeoteleuton can account for the shorter readings).

F. Doctrinal Changes

Example. 1 John 5:7–8: This "Heavenly Witnesses" passage has no nonsuspect Greek manuscript support.

Appendix 2

Text Types and Groupings of Witnesses

In order to segregate witnesses to the New Testament text into the various text types, you will need to be familiar with the following tables of witnesses. As noted in Chapter 2, the existence of the Caesarean text type is highly doubtful. Witnesses once thought to belong to this text type are here listed as "Other Important Witnesses."

1. The Byzantine Text Type

Gospels

A E F G H K M P S U V W (in Matthew and Luke 8:13–24:53) Y Γ Δ (except in Mark) Ψ Ω (and most minuscules) Gothic Syriac Peshitta Chrysostom

Acts

> H L P S (and most minuscules) Gothic Syriac Peshitta Chrysostom

Pauline Epistles

> K L P S 0142 (and most minuscules) Gothic Syriac Peshitta Chrysostom

General Epistles

> H K L S 42 398 (and most minuscules) Gothic Syriac Peshitta Chrysostom

Apocalypse

> Q 046 82 93 429 469 808 920 2048

2. The Alexandrian Text Type

Gospels

> p^{66} p^{75} (and most other papyri to some extent) ℵ (though somewhat "Western," esp. in John 1:1–8:38) B C L T W (in Luke 1–8:12; John 5:12 to end) X Z Δ (in Mark) Ξ Ψ (in Mark; partially in Luke and John) 059 0162 20 33 81 164 215 376 579 718 850 892 1241 1739 Sahidic Bohairic Clement Origen Didymus

Acts

> p^{45} p^{50} p^{74} ℵ A B C Ψ 048 076 096 6 33 81 104 326 1175

Pauline Epistles

> p^{46} ℵ A B C H I M P Ψ 048 081 088 0220 6 33 81 104 326 1175 1739 1908 Sahidic Bohairic

General Epistles

> p^{20} p^{23} p^{72} ℵ A B C P Ψ 048 056 0142 0156 0167 6 33 81 89 104 323 1175 1739 2298

Apocalypse

> p^{47} ℵ A C P 0169 0207 61 69 94 241 254 1006 1175 1611 1841 1852 2040 2344 2351

3. The Western Text Type
Gospels

p^{25} p^{37} ℵ (in John 1:1–8:38) D W (in Mark 1:1–5:30) 0177 (in Luke 22:44–56, 61–63) Old Latin Vulgate Sinaitic Syriac Curetonian Syriac Tertullian Irenaeus Marcion Cyprian Augustine Ambrosiaster

Acts

p^{29} p^{38} p^{41} p^{48} D E 066 1 36 255 257 338 383 440 614 913 1108 1245 1518 1611 1739 1874 2138 2298 Old Latin Vulgate Early Latin Fathers

Pauline Epistles

D E F G 88 181 915 917 1836 1898 1912 Old Latin Vulgate Early Latin Fathers Syrian Fathers to ca. A.D. 450

General Epistles

D E Old Latin Vulgate Irenaeus Tertullian Cyprian Augustine

Apocalypse

F Old Latin

4. Other Important Witnesses (sometimes called "Caesarean" Witnesses)

p^{37} p^{45} (in Mark) W (in Mark 5:31–16:8) Θ 0188 Family 1 (= 1 22 118 131 209 872 1278 1582 2193) Family 13 (= 13 69 124 174 230 346 543 788 828 983 1689) 28 157 565 700 1071 1275 1604 Georgian Armenian Palestinian Syriac Eusebius Cyril-Jerusalem

Appendix 3

A Worksheet for New Testament Textual Criticism

The following worksheet is provided as a general guideline for conducting a complete textual analysis. Provide as much information as possible on your own, formulate your own conclusions, and then check these against the conclusions of the experts. Consult the tables of witnesses in Appendix 2 for help on matters pertaining to external evidence.

I. **Preliminaries**
   A. Biblical Reference:
   B. Greek text involved in variation as found in UBS[4]:
   C. Literal Rendering:
   D. NRSV Rendering:
   E. NKJV Rendering:
   F. Delineation of Problem:

1. List any alternative readings.
2. Label each alternative as to the kind of variation is involved (e.g., omission, addition, transposition of words, substitution).
3. Translate the alternatives so as to bring out the differences in meaning that each conveys.

Alternative Readings	Kind of Variation	Translation

II. External Evidence
A. Accumulation of Evidence.
   1. List readings.
   2. Record the evidence for each from UBS[4].

Readings	Evidence

B. Distribution of Evidence. Segregate the support for each reading into the various text types.

Readings	Byzantine	Alexandrian	Western	Others

C. Evaluation of Evidence. Arrange the readings in descending order of probability with the "better attested" reading at the top. Explain why each reading is assigned its particular position.

Readings	Rationale

III. Internal Evidence

A. Transcriptional Probabilities. Test each of the variants in the light of known types of scribal errors (see Appendix 1).

Readings	Possible Error in Transcription

B. Intrinsic Probabilities. Examine each variant from the standpoint of the author's style, vocabulary, and theology.

Readings	Author's Style	Vocabulary	Theology

C. Evaluation. Arrange the variants in descending order of preference on the basis of internal evidence.

Readings	Rationale

IV. Summary and Conclusion

Give an overall summary evaluating all areas of investigation and stating your conclusion with regard to the textual problem.

Select Bibliography

The works listed below can be read with profit and relative ease by the beginning student. Some works are given a brief evaluation that is necessarily subjective.

Aland, Kurt and Barbara. *The Text of the New Testament.* 2d ed. Trans. by Erroll F. Rhodes. Grand Rapids: Eerdmans, 1989. The most recent introductory work, ably but somewhat dogmatically presented.

Black, David Alan. "Conjectural Emendations in the Gospel of Matthew." *Novum Testamentum* 31 (1989): 1– 15.

———. "Jesus on Anger: The Text of Matthew 5:22a Revisited." *Novum Testamentum* 30 (1988): 1–8.

———. "The Peculiarities of Ephesians and the Ephesian Address." *Grace Theological Journal* 2 (1981): 59–73.

———. "The Text of John 3:13." *Grace Theological Journal* 6 (1985): 49–66.

Comfort, Philip W. *Early Manuscripts and Modern Translations of the New Testament.* Wheaton: Tyndale, 1990. Description and criticism of the early papyri and several English translations.

Epp, Eldon J. "Textual Criticism." In *The New Testament and Its Modern Interpreters.* Ed. by E. J. Epp and G. W. Macrae. Atlanta: Scholars Press, 1989. Pp. 75–126. Outlines in great detail advances in textual criticism since World War II.

Fee, Gordon D. "The Textual Criticism of the New Testament." In *The Expositor's Bible Commentary*. Ed. by F. E. Gaebelein. Grand Rapids: Zondervan, 1979. Vol. 1. Pp. 419–33.

Finegan, Jack. *Encountering New Testament Manuscripts*. Grand Rapids: Eerdmans, 1974. Excellent introduction, with stress on reader involvement.

Greenlee, J. Harold. *Introduction to New Testament Textual Criticism*. Grand Rapids: Eerdmans, 1964. A fine standard work, somewhat outdated but still good reading.

———. *Scribes, Scrolls, and Scripture*. Grand Rapids: Eerdmans, 1985. Highly recommended for lay people.

Hodges, Zane C., and Farstad, A. L., eds. *The Greek New Testament According to the Majority Text*. Nashville: Nelson, 1982. A deft if somewhat dogmatic defense of the Byzantine text type.

Holmes, Michael W. "Textual Criticism." In *New Testament Criticism and Interpretation*. Ed. by D. A. Black and D. S. Dockery. Grand Rapids: Zondervan, 1991. Pp. 99–134. Good, up-to-date coverage of subject matter and methodology.

Metzger, Bruce M. *A Textual Commentary on the Greek New Testament*. New York: United Bible Societies, 1971. Gives the rationale for the readings printed in the *Greek New Testament*.

———. *The Text of the New Testament*. 3d rev. ed. Oxford: University Press, 1992. The standard textbook.

Sturz, Harry A. *The Byzantine Text-type and New Testament Textual Criticism*. Nashville: Nelson, 1984. Advocates the usefulness (but not primacy) of the Byzantine text type.

Westcott, B. F., and Hort, F. J. A. *The New Testament in the Original Greek*, [ii] *Introduction* [and] *Appendix*. Cambridge: Macmillan, 1881. Excellent description of textual criticism up to the time of writing.

Scripture Index

Subject Index

Subject Index